Northumberland Street, WC2, may seem a strange location for an inn named (in 1957) after the fictional detective from Baker Street, but it has connections with Sherlock Holmes. Sir Henry Baskerville stayed in the Northumberland Hotel and it was to another Hotel on Northumberland Avenue that Holmes traced the criminal in 'The Adventure of the Noble Bachelor'. The tavern is filled with Holmes memorabilia and upstairs is a remarkably precise reconstruction of his room at 221B Baker Street. The portrait of the detective bears a striking resemblance to the actor Peter Cushing, who memorably played the role of the detective on several occasions.

LONDON INN SIGNS

Dominic Rotheroe

Shire Publications Ltd

CONTENTS

Copyright © 1990 by Dominic Rotheroe. First published 1990. Shire Album 257. ISBN 0 7478 0088 X.

Printed in Great Britain by C. I. Thomas & Sons (Haverfordwest) Ltd, Press Buildings, Merlins Bridge, Haverfordwest, Dyfed SA61 1XF.

British Library Cataloguing in Publication Data: Rotheroe, Dominic. London inn signs. 1. London. Inn signs. I. Title. 659. 1342. ISBN 0-7478-0088-X.

Cover: *The Rising Sun Inn in Cloth Fair, EC1 (Cadbury Lamb).*

The George in Borough High Street, SE1, is the last of the old galleried coaching inns in London and still gives some idea of how such taverns used to look. Shakespeare, Dr Johnson and Dickens are thought to have drunk beneath the sign of St George, but the present building dates from after the first was destroyed by fire in 1677.

Left: *The Hoop and Grapes in Aldgate, EC3, claims to be the oldest inn in London. It survived the Great Fire and divides the parish of St Mary's, Whitechapel, from that of St Botolph's, Aldgate. The sign is derived from the old emblem of a wreath of vine leaves which was used to advertise an inn.*

Centre: *The Angel in Thayer Street, W1, has an elaborate advertisement of which the medieval church would not have disapproved, as the churchwardens were often the local brewers.*

Right: *The Three Tuns or barrels, seen here in Jewry Street, EC3, is derived from the arms of the Vintners' Company and was a popular sign indicating that wine and beer were sold within.*

ORIGINS

'A great open-air portrait gallery' is how one writer referred to the thousands of inn signs hanging all over Great Britain and it is in London that this exhibition is at its most intensive and varied. Much about the past, and often the present, of the different communities which constitute London can be learned from their inn signs. Sometimes this is easy — *The Printer's Devil* off Fleet Street, EC4, has obvious connections with its surroundings — but often the associations are obscure: the odd coupling *Bull and Mouth*, for instance, is a corruption of 'Boulogne Mouth', the harbour of the French city whose capture by Henry VIII is celebrated by several signs.

Such corruptions are quite appropriate for it was to guide the illiterate that shop and inn signs were set up. In former times when few could read the only sure way of proclaiming one's trade was to use an emblem, which in the case of the first taverns was a bush of vine leaves, a natural enough device derived from ancient Rome, where signboards were common — no less than nine hundred were found in the ruins of Herculaneum. Reference to this bush gave rise to the saying 'A good wine needs no bush', and its influence is still to be found in signs such as *The Hoop and Grapes* in Aldgate, EC3, the hoop having formerly provided the framework for the wreath of leaves which made the sign.

Left: *The exterior of The Black Friar at the north end of Blackfriars Bridge, EC4, is decorated with many signs and carvings of the friars enjoying their drink. The area is named after a Dominican monastery which stood there from the thirteenth century until the Dissolution in 1536. The monks wore black habits.*

Right: *The monastery of the Friars of the Holy Cross stood near Ye Old Crutched Friars on Crosswall, EC3. The friars had red crosses ('crouches' in Middle English) embroidered on their habits and became known as the Crutched Friars.*

RELIGIOUS SIGNS

As competition increased, it became necessary to distinguish between different inns by using individual signs, each vying with the others for the attention of the public. This public consisted principally of travellers, as an inn was a place of accommodation as well as refreshment, and in medieval times the majority of travellers were pilgrims. Their need for lodgings at holy places led to a long-standing connection between churches and breweries, which in many towns were sited next to each other, with the church-warden acting as brewer, fermenting liquor for the 'ale frolics' at which church funds were raised. It is appropriate that the inn first appears in English literature in Chaucer's *The Canterbury Tales*, where the pilgrims gathered at the now defunct *Tabard* in Southwark.

The pilgrim trade also gave rise to hundreds of religious signs, probably de-signed with the dual purpose of luring the devout and acknowledging the source of the inn's main revenue. In London the most famous of these was *The Angel*, Islington, N1, after which the under-ground station was named, and where travellers to the city would stop for the night rather than venture the rest of the way in the dark.

The St John of Jerusalem in St John Street, EC1, is named after the church and hospital built in Jerusalem after the First Crusade and the religious nursing order founded as a consequence. The Knights Hospitallers of St John cared for sick pilgrims and were the forerunners of today's St John Ambulance Brigade. By the time it was disbanded during the Reformation the order had become one of the most powerful in Europe, but all that remains now of their London headquarters is the gatehouse nearby which houses a museum about the Order of St John.

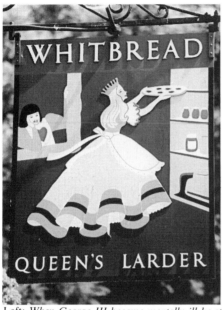

Left: *When George III became mentally ill he stayed for a while in Queen Square, Bloomsbury, WC1, under the care of a Dr Willis. Queen Charlotte rented an underground cellar in a nearby inn where she stored food and drink for him, and afterwards the pub was renamed The Queen's Larder.*

Right: *Many people used a white horse as an emblem or heraldic badge, including the Saxons, the county of Kent, the Earls of Arundel and the House of Hanover. This sign in Hoxton Street, N1, is derived from the crown of Henry VI. It is described heraldically as 'a horse crined and unguled argent, gorged with a coronet of crosses paty and fleurs-de-lis, a chain affixed thereto'.*

ROYAL AND HERALDIC SIGNS

In 1393 Richard II made it compulsory for an inn to display a sign and fittingly it was his heraldic badge which inspired one of Britain's most popular signs, *The White Hart*, popularly supposed to be the stag which Alexander the Great is said to have caught and adorned with a gold collar. Many popular animal signs derive from heraldic details or badges and, being more distinctive, these are far more widespread than signs showing an entire coat of arms, which was more elaborate and frequently similar to several others. In medieval times they appeared in profusion as many innkeepers were former stewards of great families and wished to proclaim their allegiance — a *Bear and Ragged Staff*, for instance, indicated the Earls of Warwick, a *Green Dragon* those of Pembroke. Self-interest,

however, often prevailed over loyalty and during the Wars of the Roses, when the succession to the throne was uncertain, many *King's Head* and *Rose* inns frequently changed face and colour in the hope of appearing to support whichever house was currently more powerful.

Meanwhile inn signs became ever larger in their bid for custom, often spanning the entire width of the street. These were known as gallows or beam signs. The White Hart in Scole, Norfolk, erected a huge one at the cost of £1000 which included 25 lifesize figures. In streets as narrow as those in the City of London such signs, as well as blocking out much of the light from above, became increasingly dangerous to those passing below so that in 1667 it was decreed that 'in all the streets no signboard shall hang

6

across'. This, however, did not stop them from expanding vertically and becoming so heavy that in 1712 one fell down in Fleet Street taking the front of a house with it and killing four passers-by.

Right: The swan was a popular symbol, used as a royal badge by Henry IV, Edward III and Edward IV, and in coats of arms including that of the Vintners' Company. It may also have been used as an inn sign because of its association with liquid, as seen in this verse from an Irish tavern: 'This is the Swan that dips her neck in water,/Why not we as well as she, drink plenty of (Beamish and Crawford's) porter.' This sign is in Fetter Lane, EC4.

Below left: The New Red Lion in St John Street, EC1, is a modern variation on one of Britain's most popular signs. Most Red Lions derive from the heraldic badge of John of Gaunt (1340-99), who for thirty years was the most powerful man in England.

Below right: Castles are associated with food, shelter and security, and it is not surprising that many pubs took the name of The Castle. Sometimes the sign was taken from the emblem for Castile, which indicated that Spanish wines were sold within. The Castle in Battersea High Street, SW11, used to display a sign carved from a solid piece of wood in the reign of Elizabeth I when the first tavern was built there. As the sign became popular, innkeepers chose the name of one particular castle such as The Pontefract Castle in Wigmore Street, W1.

Left: *The London Stone in Cannon Street, EC4, refers to one of London's most ancient relics, a stone in the building next door which some believe marked the point from which the Romans measured distances from the city but which others think has a Saxon origin. It has been moved three times, most recently after the Second World War. The first Lord Mayor lived nearby and the sign portrays Dick Whittington (1358-1423), who, when Mayor, successfully prosecuted the Brewers' Company for overcharging on their ale.*

Right: *The Running Footman in Charles Street, Mayfair, W1, is the only sign in Britain which remembers the exhausting job of the servant who had to run ahead of his master's coach to warn of his approach and pay tollkeepers. Many running footmen served residents of Mayfair and could sometimes run an astonishing 20 miles (32 km) in two hours. According to Sir Walter Scott, the footman depicted on the sign attended the coach of John, Earl of Hopetoun.*

TRANSPORT AND TRAVEL SIGNS

After the seventeenth century the main influences on inns and their signs were the successive innovations in transport. The dawn of the coaching era in the early eighteenth century, when travel on a relatively ambitious scale became possible for the first time, instilled new vigour into the trade, with more and more travellers requiring accommodation and refreshment along the main routes. As services improved and growing numbers of people took to the roads (two million in 1825) thousands of inns depended entirely on the custom from coaches. In the end the trades of coaching and innkeeping became so intertwined that, apart from the mail coaches, the entire coaching industry was owned and run by innkeepers. The era of coaching inns, along with the shorter heyday of those taverns which had sprung up alongside the busy canals, came to an end with the advent of the railways. This nearly emptied the roads and caused many country taverns to close, although some kept going until the motor car brought traffic back on to the roads.

Inn signs kept pace with these changes as shrewdly as they had done with changes in the monarchy. Few signs depicting pre-coach travel survive: *The Two Chairmen* in Dartmouth Street, SW1,

Above left: *While Queen Anne was having her portrait painted by Sir James Thornhill in his studio in Dean Street, W1, her sedan-chair bearers patronised the tavern opposite and are remembered on its sign.*

Above right: *If, in the days before street numbering, one did not have a sign, one could always make one's house more distinctive by painting a part of it. Blue-painted posts seem to have been popular in the West End and at this inn in Bennet Street, SW1, they were used to advertise a fleet of sedan chairs plying for hire in the street.*

Below left: *The Viaduct Tavern opposite the Old Bailey in Newgate Street, EC1, pictures on both sides of its two signboards four different scenes of the same view of Holborn Viaduct. The Viaduct was constructed in 1867 to span the Holebourne, from which the area gets its name.*

Below right: *Like so many inns named after railways, The Railway Tavern by Liverpool Street station, EC2, has made itself a place of historic record by displaying, along with other railwayana, the crests of the 25 railway companies which amalgamated to form the Great Eastern Railway, itself to become part of the London and North Eastern Railway in 1923.*

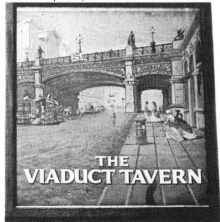

9

THE
ANTIGALLICAN

and *The Blue Posts*, Bennet Street, SW1, advertising sedan chairs, are two examples. The coaches brought with them a plethora of related signs — in London at one time there were 52 *Coach and Horses*. Other inns were named after specific coaches, like *The Flying Dutchman* in Camberwell, various *Rest and Be Thankful* inns and *The Perseverance*, probably named after a stage-coach, in Shroton Street, NW1, testify to how arduous journeys over the poor roads could be. When the railways arrived many inns again updated their signs. Despite the predominance of the motor car some of these have been retained as historical records, although others have been changed and a few have been cleverly modernised: *The Railway Tavern* in Watford simply replaced its steam engine with the London Underground symbol.

London was long one of the world's major seaports and this connection is not neglected by inn signs. The oldest riverside pub, The Prospect of Whitby, on Wapping Wall, E1, dates from 1520 and was named after a ship which used to moor nearby. Also named after a ship is the Antigallican (above) in Tooley Street, SE1. The Antigallican was a British warship in the Napoleonic Wars and its name means 'anti-French'. The Ship and Compass (below left) in London Street, EC3, has a large three-dimensional sign. The Friend at Hand in Herbrand Street, WC1, shows a lifeboat coxswain rescuing a drowning seaman. The Old Father Thames (below right) on the Albert Embankment, SE1, pays tribute to the river which gave the city its importance.

OLD FATHER THAMES

The Chelsea Potter in Kings Road, SW3, was renamed in 1958 in honour of David Rawnsley, who founded the Chelsea Pottery nearby. Some of Rawnsley's work decorates the inn.

SIGNS OF TRADES

Before houses were numbered shop and trade signs were essential if customers who were not local were to find a place of commerce. Those without signs had to resort to the most convoluted advertising, relying on the signs of others — 'At her house, *The Red Ball and Acorn*, over against *The Glove Tavern* in Queen Street, Cheapside, near *The Three Crowns*, liveth a Gentlewoman . . .' *et cetera*. The introduction of street numbering in 1805, along with the spread of literacy, ended the need for pictorial shop signs and, though many were retained

11

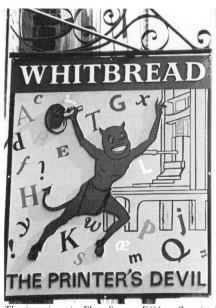

The inn signs in Fleet Street, EC4, reflect its importance as the former centre of the newspaper industry. In the trade the errand boy was called the printer's devil and, like the demon on the sign in Fetter Lane, EC4, he was often blamed for any confusion in the text. The Cartoonist in Shoe Lane, EC4, is a modern pub and the headquarters of the Cartoonist Club. It is the only inn to change its sign every year, each time using a drawing by the current 'Cartoonist of the Year'. At The Witness Box in Tudor Street, EC4, next to the Inns of Court, the annual 'Witness Box Awards' for the best crime reporting of the year used to be held. The Punch Tavern, Fleet Street, EC4, was so named because Punch and Judy shows were held nearby. The founders of the humorous magazine 'Punch' thought up the idea while drinking here and named it after the pub.

through affection, they have gradually disappeared, but the numerous inn signs associated with trade are a reminder of them. Many inns took their names from the dominant trade of the surrounding area, hoping to attract thirsty workers, and also provided the setting for more

Above: *The Hand and Shears in Smithfield, EC1, is over four hundred years old and it was here that the Lord Mayor used to open the Bartholomew Fair by cutting the first piece of cloth to be sold, a custom which is reflected in ribbon-cutting ceremonies now held when a new supermarket or such-like is opened. The fair, which lasted from 1133 until its suppression in 1855, was a rowdy and licentious free-for-all and was missed by few when it ceased.*

Top right: *The Turners' Arms in Crawford Street, W1, is an example of an armorial sign displaying the arms of a craft guild, in this case the Worshipful Company of the Turners of London, chartered in 1604.*

Right: *The word 'jolly', meaning good or admirable, rarely appears on signboards these days as the workers referred to thought it vulgar and preferred the word 'arms'. The Jolly Gardeners is still to be seen in several places, though, and this one is in Cobourg Street, NW1, near Euston station.*

The Glassblower and Glasshouse Street, W1, in which the pub stands, are both named after a large glassworks which once operated there.

formal meetings — many clubs, societies and unions have been founded over a glass of ale.

Around Smithfield meat market, EC1, are *The Smithfield Tavern*, *The Old Red Cow* and *The Hand and Shears*, all with a special dispensation, like inns near the other wholesale markets, to serve market workers (but not the public) between 6.30 and 9 o'clock in the morning.

Many heraldic devices from the arms of trade associations can be found on inn signs. Some of the more famous are *The Elephant and Castle*, which was taken from the Cutlers Company, who sometimes used ivory in their knife handles; *The Lamb and Flag*, which represented the Merchant Taylors, whose guild developed from a religious fraternity of St John the Baptist, who is represented in heraldry by a Paschal or Holy Lamb which carries a cross and pennant; and *The Three Compasses*, which signified the Carpenters' Company of London.

Left: The sign outside The London Apprentice in Old Street, EC1, depicts a modern equivalent of the apprentices who patronised the pub in times past.

Right: The two symbols of the Crown and Shuttle on Shoreditch High Street, E7, refer to the former royal landownership in the area and the local weaving industry. From the late sixteenth century, first Flemish and later Huguenot Protestant refugees from religious persecution settled in Spitalfields, bringing new expertise to the industry, which flourished in the area until the mid nineteenth century, when it began to decline.

Ye Olde Cock Tavern in Fleet Street, EC4, with its original gilded bird said to have been carved by the great sculptor and wood-carver Grinling Gibbons, was frequented by famous literary and theatrical men such as Goldsmith, Sheridan, Garrick, Irving and Pepys. Here the aging Dickens had his last dinner in public and Tennyson even referred to it in a poem: 'O plump head-waiter at the Cock/To which I most resort/How goes the time? " 'Tis five o'clock"/Go fetch a pint of port.' The original tavern was sited on the other side of the road and the present building dates from 1887.

THE ARTS

The arts are better represented on inn signs in London than anywhere else. Several well known artists have painted pub signs. The most famous of these was William Hogarth, whose *Man with a Load of Mischief* once hung in Oxford Street, W1, depicting a weary man with a drunken woman and a monkey on his back. Others who have contributed to the gallery include Sir Godfrey Kneller, George Morland, David Cox and the celebrated carver Grinling Gibbons, who did a sign for *Ye Olde Cock Tavern* in Fleet Street, EC4.

The Shakespeare's Head in Great Marlborough Street, W1, is a good example of a widespread sign. Sir John Falstaff, every landlord's favourite customer, is one of the most popular Shakespearean characters. The Macbeth in Hoxton Street, N1, is perhaps an odd name for an inn, considering that bad luck is ascribed to the name by the theatrical profession. One of the pub's walls has a display of scenes from the play.

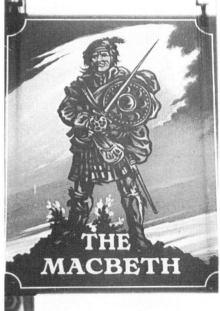

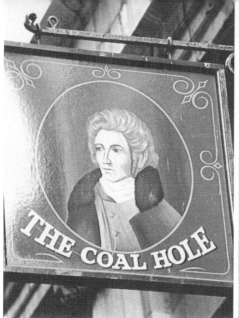

Many London inns have long-standing connections with the theatre. The Coal Hole on the Strand, WC2, gets its name from the coal-heavers who loaded lighters on the Thames in the early nineteenth century and refreshed themselves here, but, as the sign shows, it is best known as a haunt of the famous actor Edmund Kean (1789-1833), who founded a club for repressed husbands here. Further down the road is The Lyceum on Wellington Street, WC2. It stands next to the erstwhile theatre of the same name and the actor shown making up on the sign is Sir Henry Irving, who leased the theatre from 1871 to 1898 and gave some of his most memorable performances there. In 1895 he became the first actor to receive a knighthood. Around the corner from this in Drury Lane, WC2, is the Nell of Old Drury, which refers to Nell Gwynne, the orange-seller, mistress of Charles II and popular comedienne at the Theatre Royal opposite. At one time she lived near The Pindar of Wakefield in Kings Cross Road, WC1, which is said to have had an underground passage linked to her house. This inn is now called The Water Rats after the Grand Order of Water Rats, the charity run by variety entertainers. This was founded in 1889 and was christened after a bedraggled pony, nicknamed Water Rat, which belonged to the founder.

Songs and ballads have been the inspiration behind quite a few signs. The opening lines from the famous music-hall song *Nellie Dean*,

'There's an old mill by the stream, Nellie Dean,
Where we used to sit and dream, Nellie Dean . . .',

are visualised on a sign of the same name in Dean Street, W1. The *Hearts of Oak* in Dock Street, E1, which used

Right: *Ye Olde Cheshire Cheese in Fleet Street, EC4, rebuilt after the Great Fire of 1666, is one of the most famous pubs in London. Dr Samuel Johnson lived nearby and was one of many illustrious customers. Others over the years have included Pope, Thackeray, Conan Doyle, Voltaire and Dickens. Some of them performed the ceremony of making the first cut in Ye Pudding, which weighed between 50 and 80 pounds (23-36 kg), on the first Monday in October.*

Below: *The lone piper depicted on this sign in Blackfriars Road, SE1, is playing the lament 'The Flowers of the Forest', which is played by all Scottish regiments. As the lament draws to a close the piper gradually retreats, the sound dying away. This tradition is said to have stemmed from the battle of Flodden, on 9th September 1513, when King James IV of Scotland and the flower of the Scottish nobility, slain by the English army, were similarly mourned by a single piper.*

to cater for old seamen from a home nearby, takes its name from a sailors' song. On the other hand, *The Eagle* in the City found its way into a famous rhyme:

'Up and down the City Road,
In and out *The Eagle*,
That's the way the money goes,
Pop goes the weasel.'

The art most often represented on inn signs, however, is literature, for the taverns of London were frequented by many of the great writers of earlier centuries, such as Dr Johnson, Oliver Goldsmith, Alexander Pope, William Congreve and W. M. Thackeray. Shakespeare and his characters can be seen on signs throughout Britain and he is believed to have known *The Raglan* (formerly *The Bush*) in Aldersgate, EC1, *The Cockpit* on St Andrews Hill, EC4, and *The Anchor*, Bankside, SE1.

Above: *Even film stars are represented on inn signs. The Charlie Chaplin is on the New Kent Road, SE1, near the birthplace in Kennington of the silent clown (1889-1977).*

Right: *The Walrus and the Carpenter on Lovat Lane, EC3, has a sign taken from one of John Tenniel's famous illustrations for 'Alice in Wonderland'. It is near the former site of Billingsgate Market, which moved to Docklands in 1982, and in earlier times, when the pub was known as The Cock, the fish porters were allowed to drink there out of hours.*

The Betsey in Farringdon Road, EC1, is named after Betsey Trotwood, David's great aunt in Charles Dickens's 'David Copperfield'. The Artful Dodger in Royal Mint Street, E1, gets its name from Fagin's nimble child thief in 'Oliver Twist'. There are surprisingly few inns bearing Dickens's own name. The Dickens Inn at St Katharine's Dock, E1, is popular with tourists and was opened in 1976 by the writer's great grandson. Dickensian cabarets are held in the Dickens Room upstairs and the ground-floor bar serves only real, un-bottled ale.

But it is Charles Dickens who is most associated with and was the best publicist of London's inns and their atmosphere. Many of them found their way into his novels, including *The Prospect of Whitby* on Wapping Wall, E1 (in *Our Mutual Friend*), *The Red Lion* in Parliament Street, SW1 (in *David Copperfield*), and *The Crown* in Brewer Street, W1 (in *Nicholas Nickleby*), and he was a regular customer at many more. The taverns in return have decorated many of their signs with his characters.

Left: *The Intrepid Fox in Wardour Street, W1, refers not to a cunning animal but to the eighteenth-century politician Charles James Fox (1749-1806), the great rival of William Pitt. He opposed the war with France and was about to introduce a bill for the abolition of slavery when he died. A former landlord of this pub was a great supporter of his.*

Right: *The Independent in Bingfield Street, N1, is named in honour of Louis Kossuth (1802-94), leader of the 1849 Hungarian revolution against the Hapsburgs, the Austrian rulers of his country. He was defeated and eventually came to Britain, where he was enthusiastically received and addressed demonstrations in Copenhagen Fields, next to which the inn now stands. He lived most of his life in exile.*

FAMOUS PEOPLE

Although it is rare these days, inn signs were quick to acknowledge a hero of the hour, even if it meant discarding a long-held portrait in favour of the new celebrity. When a politician was depicted on the hanging sign there might often be the ulterior motive of hoping to attract drinkers of the same political persuasion, but generally it was simply a way for an innkeeper to show whom he admired. As new favourites emerged the now less familiar hero of yesteryear might be discarded in his turn. Figures such as Nelson and Wellington (the two most popular signs in this category) are still famous and appear in almost every large town, but some signs to lesser known celebrities of the past still survive.

The Marquis of Granby, Commander-in-Chief during the Seven Years War, is still popular, probably because he is said to have paid off his non-commissioned

The Clarence in Dover Street, W1, commemorates the fate of George, Duke of Clarence (1449-78), who is said to have been drowned in a butt of malmsey in the Tower of London on the orders of his brother, the future Richard III.

Baron Morrison of Lambeth (1888-1965) was a distinguished political figure during the early and mid twentieth century. From being an errand boy, Herbert Morrison went on to help found the London Labour Party, become leader of the London County Council and hold high office in both the wartime cabinet under Churchill and the post-war Attlee government. On this sign in Wandsworth Road, SW8, he is seen as depicted by David Low, the famous cartoonist.

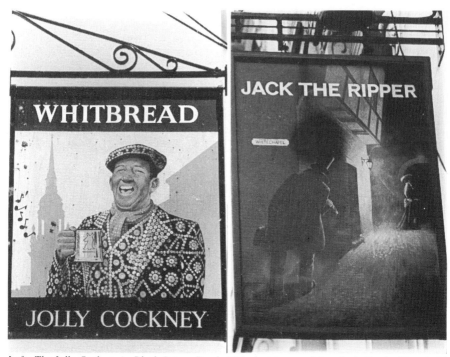

Left: *The Jolly Cockney in Black Prince Road, SE1, depicts one of London's Pearly Kings in his suit encrusted with pearl buttons. Nearby in the Lambeth Walk one can see photographs of numerous Pearly Kings and Queens.*

Right: *London's most notorious killer is remembered at the Jack the Ripper in Commercial Street, E1. This area of Whitechapel was terrorised in 1888 by the brutal murder of five prostitutes. The killer, who was never caught, became known as Jack the Ripper. Inside the pub there are newspaper clippings and photographs of the places where the killings occurred.*

officers with a gratuity to be used for buying an inn on their retirement.

Another great commander was *Admiral Codrington*, who gave his name to inns on Mossop Street, SW3, and New Church Road, SE5. He joined the navy at the age of thirteen and led a squadron at Trafalgar but was best known for his part in the destruction of the Turkish navy at Navarino in 1827.

The Hero of Switzerland in Brixton, SW2, pays tribute to William Tell, the saviour of his native district in Switzer-land, who was captured by his enemies and in a famous episode had to shoot an apple off his son's head.

There are few signs commemorating the illustrious of the twentieth century, but there used to be a *John Baird* in north London in honour of the pioneer of television, who first demonstrated his invention in Frith Street, W1, in 1926, and there is a *Henry Cooper* in the Old Kent Road, SE1, named after the famous boxer by the landlord, himself a former pugilist.

Left: *The Beehive is a popular sign, perhaps used to indicate a lively and interesting pub, though originally intended to represent industry. This one is in Crawford Street, W1.*

Right: *In medieval times there was an annual Festival of the Popinjay, which is a parrot. At the festival archers would shoot at a dummy bird on a pole and the winner was dubbed Captain Popinjay. A popinjay also formed part of the arms of the Abbots of Cirencester, whose house once stood on the site of the modern inn in Fleet Street, EC4.*

ANIMAL SIGNS

There are probably more signs of animals than there are of any other category. Most of these are either heraldic or symbols of some sort, like *The Poppinjay* in Fleet Street, EC4, which was the sign of the Abbots of Cirencester, whose house once stood on the present inn's site. Many animals, though, are there in their own right and the variety is enormous, ranging from insects to monsters. Lions and bears apart, British wildlife is naturally the most popular, but several exotic species are represented — there is a *Giraffe* in Penton Place, SE17, a *Panther* in Bethnal Green, E2, and a *Tiger* on Tower Hill, EC3. The latter inn provided meals for Elizabeth I when she was imprisoned in the Tower and preserves a mummified cat with which she is said to have played.

Other animals have earned their places through cruel sports: bull-baiting, bear-baiting, cock-fighting and various forms of hunting. One of the lesser known of these sports is shown on *The Dog and Duck* in Soho, W1 (a district which de-

Above left: *The griffin is an heraldic creature with the body, hind legs and tail of a lion, and the head, wings and claws of an eagle. Being a combination of the king of beasts and the king of birds it figures in several coats of arms, including that of the Dukes of Marlborough, and here it is seen in Villiers Street, WC2.*

Above right: *The interior of The Cockpit on St Andrews Hill, EC4, has been arranged so as to recreate the pit and gallery which formerly stood there as long ago as the sixteenth century. Cock-fighting was banned in Britain in 1849 and the inn changed its name, but it has reverted to the old one with which Shakespeare, who lived nearby, would have been familiar.*

The phoenix, a mythical demi-eagle which rose from the flames of its own funeral pyre, is sometimes used heraldically as a reference to the Seymours, Dukes of Somerset, or as a symbol of the Resurrection, but it can also indicate that the previous building on the site was burnt down. This sign can be seen in Margaret Street, W1.

rives its name from a hunting call). A duck with pinioned wings was chased around a village pond by various dogs, released one by one. If the duck were caught there were free drinks for everyone. If it eluded the dogs, their owners paid. Bets were laid on the outcome.

26

The Tom Cribb in Panton Street, SW1, was renamed in 1960 in honour of a former landlord and prizefighter who was champion of England from 1808 to 1818. His first fight, at the age of 24 lasted 76 rounds and he soon became a popular figure. At the coronation of George IV he guarded the entrance to Westminster Hall. The Ring in Blackfriars Road, SE1, has one of the few signs which explains the reason for its name.

SPORTING SIGNS

Of less violent sports cricket has inspired the most signs. There used to be a popular pub in Piccadilly, W1, called *The Yorker*. One side of the sign featured the burly W. G. Grace and on the other was the lean 6 foot 3 inch (190 cm) form of F. R. Spofforth, a bowler who in 1882 took 14 wickets for 90 runs against Australia bowling 'yorkers' that could scarcely be played.

Soccer has not had the impact on signs one would expect, especially considering the custom it brings, but at least three football clubs have inspired signs: *The Gunners*, for Arsenal, in Finsbury Park, N4; *The Hammers*, for West Ham United, in E15; and *The Spurs*, for Tottenham Hotspur, at Edmonton, N9.

The Doggett's Coat and Badge by Blackfriars Bridge, SE1, is named after the 4½ mile (7.25 km) rowing race from Chelsea to London Bridge instituted by an Irish comedian called Thomas Doggett in the seventeenth century. It takes place every July and the winner receives a scarlet coat and silver badge.

Above left: *The Hand and Racquet in Whitcomb Street, WC2, is so called because the royal tennis court, often used by Charles II, lay nearby.*

Above right: *It is surprising that there are not more signs celebrating the most popular pub game, as does The City Darts in Commercial Street, E1.*

Below: *The World Turned Upside Down in the Old Kent Road, SE1, took its name from the discovery of Australia in 1683 by William Dampier. The original signboard showed a man at the South Pole and successive ones have portrayed foxes chasing huntsmen and horses driving man-drawn carriages.*

The small statues by the entrance of Magogs in Russia Row, EC2, represent Gog and Magog, two mythical British giants who were constantly fighting. During the Lord Mayor's procession in medieval times papier-mâché statues of the two combatants, 18 feet (5.5 metres) high, would be placed as guards at the entrance to London Bridge. Inside the pub the fight is continued on a clock when models of the two giants confront each other at a quarter to every hour.

CURIOSITIES

The most memorable and appealing inn signs are usually those with a sense of humour or an interesting story behind them. *The Museum Tavern* opposite the British Museum, WC1, shows two ancient Egyptians having a drink, and *The Copper* on Tower Bridge Road, SE1, displays on one side a huge copper boiler and on the other a policeman.

Dirty Dick's in Bishopsgate, EC2, is named after Nathaniel Bentley, a wealthy dandy who lived in Leadenhall Street during the eighteenth century. On the day he was to be married, with the feast and celebrations all prepared, news came that his bride had died. It is said that Nathaniel immediately locked the room

where the feast was set out and where years later rat and mouse skeletons were found beside the empty plates, and confined himself to a life of lonely squalor. This earned him the nickname 'Dirty Dick' and perhaps a place in literary history as Miss Havisham's similarly abandoned and rotting wedding feast in *Great Expectations* is believed to have been inspired by the story.

Another pub with a fascinating past is *The Railway Tavern* in West India Dock Road, E14, known all over the world as 'Charlie Brown's'. Charlie Brown was the landlord of this inn until the early 1930s and amassed a great and valuable collection of curios from all over the

Above: *The Woodman and the Original Woodman stand within a few yards of each other on Battersea High Street, SW11, where there were once many woodcutters. The Original Woodman is the older of the two and has chosen a novel way of showing it on its sign.*

Below left: *'Shades' is an ancient word for a wine vault, here built by the Woodin family in 1863 on Bishopsgate, EC2. The ghost of a friendly cellarman is said to haunt the vaults at night and to make a neat stack of casks which have been untidily dumped.*

Below right: *The slug is not a creature commonly associated with inn signs. Here, at the Slug and Lettuce on Islington Green, N1, it has been chosen to indicate the large salad counter within.*

world given him by the many sailors who came in for a drink. These oddities included a stuffed two-headed, six-legged calf, a mummified baby and numerous antique ivories, estimated to be worth £100,000. Many of these items he hung from the ceiling of the tavern. He was a much loved character: at his funeral four carriage loads of wreaths followed the hearse and ten thousand people lined the route to bid farewell to Britain's most famous landlord.

Left: *The Albion on New Bridge Street, EC4, takes its name from an old word for Britain, probably derived from 'albus', the Latin word for white, and referring to the white cliffs of Dover. The patriot seen here standing on those cliffs is John Bull, the name given to the typical sturdy Englishman by John Arbuthnot in 1712.*

Below: *The Globe in Marylebone Road, NW1, is another inn with a patriotic sign, here indicating the ubiquity of British colonialism, although the name dates back beyond the heyday of the Empire to a time when the era of exploration made it a popular inn sign.*

Left: *Pubs called the Perseverance were usually named either after a well known stage-coach of that name which stopped at the inn or after the HMS Perseverance, a troopship of the 1850s. This sign in Pritchards Road, E2, is rare in that it is misspelt, although the name on the front of the house is not.*

Right: *World's End inns were usually so named because they stood on the very edge of a town or parish and their remote sites often earned them bad reputations as the haunt of shady characters. Such was the case for this inn on the King's Road, SW3, which dates back to the reign of Charles II. Then it was really a riverside tavern, the King's Road not yet having been laid out.*

FURTHER READING

Andere, M. *Inn Signs of England*. Chameleon, 1990.
Corballis, P. *Pub Signs*. Lennard Publishing, 1988.
Delderfield, E. R. *British Inn Signs and their Stories*. David and Charles, 1966.
Dunkling, L. and Wright, G. *A Dictionary of Pub Names*. Routledge and Kegan Paul, 1987.
Lamb, C. *Inn Signs*. Shire Publications, 1976.
Larwood, J. and Camden Hotten, J. *English Inn Signs*. Blaketon Hall, 1985.